WE HOLD ON TO WHAT WE CAN

poems

WE HOLD ON TO WHAT WE CAN

SARAH ALCOTT ANDERSON

poems

Loom Press
Lowell & Amesbury
Massachusetts
2021

Loom Press, P.O. Box 1394, Lowell, MA 01853

& 15 Atlantic View, Amesbury, MA 01913

www.loompress.com

info@loompress.com

Design: Dennis Ludvino, dludvino@gmail.com

Printing: King Printing, Co., Inc., Lowell, MA

Cover photograph: Sarah Alcott Anderson

Author photograph: Jennifer Almquist

For Ben, Aengus, and Ariana

CONTENTS

ONE
Beginnings & Tornadoes

FOUR
Kaleidoscope

A NOTE FROM THE AUTHOR

Thank you, in advance, for the time you spend with these pages. Each moment of life is precious — each breath — and I cherish yours.

Some of these poems grew up alongside my children while others only just turned off the dirt road and arrived. I remember my son at two, clinging to me as I tucked him into bed; I remember tricking him into letting me go by coaching him to say, "Go be a good girl, Mama, and do your writing." Brewed over a twelve-year period, this poetry reckons with my preoccupations with family, place, loss, and longing. I wrote some of these poems for my younger self, some as a way to capture today, and others for a stranger, lifetimes from now.

I remember telling Gaby Calvocoressi, my brilliant graduate school professor, that I feared my subject matter was "too safe." Her response: "No, there is nothing more charged and dangerous than marriage and children and sheep." This line in a letter became what I would later look back on as affirmation — the kind I would pretend I didn't need, and then be direct with myself, and realize I did need it.

A line in one of my poems reads, "Be mindful of the daffodils. We're not going to be here again." In mostly plainspoken poems,

I explore interior and exterior landscapes—from childhood to motherhood, New England to Ireland—in the hopes of honoring that we *are* here right now.

You are here. Thank you, reader, for exploring these trails & hidden coves with me. I hope they speak to the humanity we share and ask more questions than provide answers. I am grateful that poetry found me when I was a girl, it still feels urgent, and it hasn't left. We hold on to what we can.

— SAA

FOREWORD

I am about to tell you something
I hope you will not forget

— FROM "CAUGHT" BY SARAH ALCOTT ANDERSON

It is a condition, not particular to America, but certainly in this country's youth-obsessed culture, that women, after they reach a certain age, are disappeared. Once they move beyond the object of lust, beyond their perceived role as muse, they are forced to fade — from film, from television, and from poetry, both as subject and as creator. There is perhaps some last light thrown on them as young mothers or aspiring professionals, but then they are set behind a veil, a kind of gauzy invisibility where the heyday in the blood is considered too tame to be of worth or notice. We see this clearly in Disney tropes where to be female is either to be the virginal princess or the old hag witch. The embattled Bellatrix or mother queen, both are little seen nor given any agency to speak, all too often relegated to the distant past by death or disappearance. But such silence cannot so easily swallow poet Sarah Alcott Anderson in her debut collection *We Hold On To What We Can*. Like a sudden summer storm, Anderson thunders against this banishment and exile, not with some enraged rattling of sabers but with raw tenderness, laughing sagacity, and an effervescent dancing spirit. In verse that seems at times spun from a sugared lightning, at other times as plain and enriched as Irish bog or New Hampshire granite, line and lyric come together to insist against a silence the world would have the poet embrace.

Writing that "before even the inkling of womanhood, // I was aware // of the sensation of losing / then finding // my body," Anderson weaves that womanhood in all that she is, as mother, lover, healer, daughter, wife, and story keeper. And yet to read this book is to know that all of these roles together cannot hold the whole that rains down in poems that are at once fierce and delicate, sweet and dangerous, full of the love, the anger, the ache, and the humor we all need to make our way in this world. Anderson's poems embody James Baldwin's notion that "History is not the past. It is the present. We carry our history with us." In these poems she is all of her life at once, managing to charge her lines with the unchecked and original energy of every experience, as if every memory was being sculpted in that moment, as if we too feel "the way my heart jumps and proves I'm alive." And so we become all at once the "girls racing headlong toward the magic / and the hurt" when "we had salt in our hair and we were fast." We are the college kid remembering the boy she knew in Ireland, "combing her finger though his hair / kicking a log into the fire / forgiving him." We are the young wife watching her husband tend to the bee box knowing "There will be honey. You / will be wonderful father." We are the mother thinking of the "audacity of this afternoon light" while holding lives together in a pandemic. We are grandmother looking back with her grandchild at the pictures and letters that spin the story of her life, insisting "Even if you're voice splinters," she says to an aged imagined self, "tell me what you can." And so we too are lit up, finding in her work the sublimity of the domestic as well as the commonality of the ecstatic.

In an early poem Anderson writes, "What I am trying to say / is that I loved you with abandon," and while in that poem the narrator is speaking to her son, it is a sentence that underscores the heart of this whole book. Here is a voice that knows just how foolishly and beautifully we live, that "these highway flares / are no more than a show. You drove / past them. We all do." The collection builds to a song, one in praise of life, in praise of love, in praise as well of all the hurt and loss that comes with having both. And it is a song against those forces that would seek to silence or diminish anyone's life. To know Sarah Alcott Anderson, to read this stunning collection, is to know her voice cannot be silenced and that these poems will never diminish.

— MATT W. MILLER

ONE

Beginnings & Tornadoes

That great cathedral space which was childhood.

— VIRGINIA WOOLF

Caution

Do not run
on this trail.
Roots, hidden stones,
and mistakes children
made a century ago
could cost you
your life. Beware
of falcons nesting.
Their giant feathers
will lead you to believe
a bridge exists.
There's only air,
only alluvium,
only silt and you alone
in this river valley.
The path bends
at the places
where you thought
they were safe,
where you left
their voices. Swinging
toward the water
could start a war.

MacMahan Island

It's just flashes that we own, little snapshots made of breath and of bone.
—JEFFREY FOUCAULT

Let me put you there:
    a small white church — MacMahan —
a Maine island — Corey's Cove. Summer congregation traipsing
    pine needles down a center aisle. *We believe.*
We're five — my sister and I — and pretend we are lost
    in the forest. A plastic spyglass — a compass

leads us away. In two years, our parents
    will separate. *All that is, seen and unseen.*
They ascend. This, before the general store
will burn, shining water,
    to the ground. *The life of the world to come.*

I still see our scuffed sneakers
with rainbow laces against the inside of the whaler.
I still see our babysitter Ala taking care of us
    those long August days
while our mother adjusts her camera lens —
    our father prepares a sermon
for the island church.

At home in winter,
    my mother's fingers turn slides
right side up in the projector — holding them
    between her eyes and the light —
then placing them one by one into their slots:
goldfinch raincoats

and cherry boots, our summer-scratched
        mosquito legs, the green
        of our moss kingdom. *Amen.*

I had heard about lost explorers — shipwrecks.
        Where were our parents
those afternoons? Just behind or ahead of us,
        I am sure. We are always turning,
responding to someone calling a name.

Drive Home

From the back seat as a girl, I watched New York City flash us to Connecticut
— tunnels, headlights, the whirl of the day— until it was lush darkness.

Earlier in the park at sundown, I'd pretended a stranger was Coco Chanel,
her bright red skirt folding in upon itself like an upside-down flower —

his lens following her everywhere. I decided I would have liked it.

Thy Kingdom Come

Every Sunday morning—
my father's left hand
holds a ballpoint pen—
circles the air just above
the page—an agitated,
tiny aircraft. It hovers
over his sermon as a pilot
squints at the sunrise.
On top of my father's
maple desk—a silver
letter opener flashes.
Once in his study—
I found yellow legal paper
in a sun patch—crumpled,
scribbled notes—a plan.
I smoothed the pages
with my small hands.
I might save these forever.
His writings covered
every inch of human passion
and potential—possibility
and hope—except
when my father's
best friend's stunt plane
went down. The lines stayed
blank—save for smudged ink—
a fingertip—an attempt.

Words to Describe Memory

If that summer has dimmed,
     is not etched,
but is a detour in fog,
        let me bring you back.
You're not ready, you say?
One evening scene, then.
I'll save the rest.

Shelter Island, a cocktail party,
my photographer mother,
her photographer friends.

I am ten, it is late July 1987, my hair
uncombed. I run barefoot
in a dress, chasing other children.
We collapse, laughing. We fall

and feel in charge
     of something. Ourselves?
     Our strong bodies? The air,
     the light, and thirty years,

     all right here, as if before even
the inkling of womanhood,

     I was aware

of the sensation of losing
     then finding
my body.

I told you: I've been anchored here
for you in that moment
hoping you'll remember.
If you're not ready,
I'll keep it safe for you.

At the Lake

Above her thick white hair,
Birch trees sun flicker.

The first time she teaches me
to break the twig and breathe it in,

I carry it for days. She always pins her hair up
loosely. The lake water blinds us.

Up the driveway, behind her house,
we bury robins' eggs — cracked,

opaque — beneath moss beds, hiding
our only treasures. At her kitchen table,

we draw houses — cross-sectioned.
Sinatra and Ellington, ingrained.

A life-sized image of her hand
beneath my son's tiny hand hangs

on my study wall. We buried the shells.
We thought they were ours.

It's About Time

It's always about time. Strings of little lights
and paper lanterns, the shimmering city over there,

the sirens over there. All those lives
in all those windows. We have to say this

headlong into the night. Here is what we say:
then she kissed me in the middle of my back.

Why didn't you call instead of getting in the pickup
in the storm? And then he left. Really left.

I still don't know, a train, I think. She put her hand
on top of my head, kissed my temple. Why

did it take us this long? My children have filled me.
They have filled me. I should have called you.

I should have told you what a poet once told me:
that it takes half a century to figure out who they are,

our real true loves. Kings and queens, at banquets,
at dances do this, in unlit places. There's a word

that means homesickness for a home that never existed,
but I remember every room in your home. We burn

into each other. Syllable, driftwood, beach fire, forest.
We throw it all on. We talk until our voices scratch

the worn wooden table, until the ocean in our story
is far away, girls racing headlong toward the magic

and the hurt. No one could have stopped us.
We had salt in our hair and we were fast.

Museum of Fine Arts, Montréal

Giacometti's figures stand as drip castles
left by children on the beach. We frown
at their feet, at crevices made by knuckles,
nails, palms. Your profile reminds me

we are wet clay—unfinished,
changeable. My stepfather builds plaster molds,
breasts and thighs of permanent earth.
Since I was seven, he has taught me

to look at the shape
of people's heads, to understand
we are feather and stone.
In my mother's art gallery, my sister and I

walked beneath wine glasses, their talk
of perspective and color. One night, a storm
darkened and silenced the room of critics.
I memorized that mass of breathing sculptures.

Twilight Water

Land stretches, and a man rows a boat across a field into the night. I hear you telling me of the forest, what you learned about yourself that summer. Just a year after the flood, you say, pointing to a wooden bench by a window. "Put your things here." I turn the vinyl over. I spin a mason jar on its side. I will always be here with your coffee, you know. I need to remind you to keep your eye on the Rose-Breasted Grosbeak or the moment will break. The headache of a siren splashes across the night. Looking down at a kid from six feet might as well be like looking up at the Milky Way. You can't bring down the solar system or those stars shooting across each other over the lake while you sleep, but you can kneel down if you are a man and a small girl stands before you, expectant. Twilight water, fiddles, flutes. I don't dream of losing teeth anymore. I don't dream of the land flooding anymore. August's tent billows from winds of every summer. Fog voices, the cove. We stand here, a frenzy of drum taps. I seal a letter with gold wax dripping into itself. I imagine you a rainforest, as distant as my great-grandmother's room. Beside her in the afternoon, I didn't want her to be ninety-four. Ceiling shadows persisted. The refrigerator droned in low shakes. Come back. I have kept time.

Caught

I am about to tell you something
I hope you will not forget. When you
were four, I built this swing for you.
I left the gate to the pasture open
when you were seven. I rebuilt the gate,
urged the sheep back into the field.
Now, you are nine. I tried but couldn't
secure the latch tonight. Animals
died. You and your sister slept,
your dreams incapable of knowing
the way a coyote can leave a sheep
in its wake. I keep seeing them out there
in the dark, replaying the primal
violence, the twisting. Earlier, I carried
each of you up steep farmhouse steps,
your limbs and eyelids heavy. Sleepily,
you recalled an evening last summer
when we lit and lofted paper lanterns
above the field where I know
wild dogs with bloodied lips
left their prey tonight.

Turning to Go

My son at three
scales a large rock.
A small climber,
without ropes
or clips, he searches
blindly, his reach
instinctual. His naked body
glows against
green-black
seaweed tumbling.
I inch forward.
He is steady. I stop.
He slips. Inch forward.
Stop. I stand behind him,
my arms ready. I imagine
holding my arms this way
for the rest of my life,
as if the space
I create with my limbs
will endure
his turning to go,
as if we ever
fully endure
someone's
turning to go.
At two in the morning
he whispers for water,
gulps, like a runner
mid-race. I kiss
his tousled hair, hot

red cheek. I hold him, boy,
not baby, all arms and legs
around me. My questions simmer:
When he's not yet eighteen...?
When he turns to me leaving...?

Thirty-Six Exposures

In his sleep, my son shouts,
"Later! Later, Snow White!
Mama?" I don't answer him.
I let him sleep. I have been
studying this contact sheet,
straining my eyes to see you.
Time has worn you away.

Prepare

I watch you kneel in moss, adjust the white bee box,
secure it in verdant ground.

        There will be honey. You
        will be a wonderful father.

It's too dark to see the spaces between stones,
yet you pile more on the wall,

        mend history. You chop wood,
        the crack of axe on stump,

the hollow ache of someone leaving.
Peeling layers off the walls

        of this two-hundred-year-old farmhouse,
        we find patterns of wood and paper

and nail that could make one cry. We hammer
into what will one day be called

        that old couple's house. You memorize
        the cry of the loon. You will be a wonderful father.

Neatly, between trees, the woodpile grows. Another bed
of earth is ready for your fingers.

        Your knuckles are ready for the soil.
        When you chop onions later in the kitchen,

you are still thinking about the bees, about the field mouse
you saw run away from us

    in terror. You entrust our garden
    to the night.

Aengus

Before I tiptoed downstairs,
I watched him breathe
next to his stuffed penguin,
inseparable kings.
In his sleep, he scolds the dog,
asks for apple juice. He might
dream of aquarium fish,
their parted lips, or the spot
on the stone wall where he sits,
tossing handfuls of grain
at the sheep. I will touch
his shaven face one day.
When he wakes now, I lift him,
giving back my stolen silence.

Traces

Which branches are not worth twisting and saving? Which ones
     should we burn?

Light pierces the narrow window, all glitter and dust. We search
     long hallways, find bead collections, notebooks,

their tiny keys. We turn a mountain trail, find traces of the animals
     that tested us, hid from us.

We are stirred into a deeper want. In Tennessee, a blue-eyed boy
     will celebrate his second birthday, face scarred by rocks in the field

where they found him one hundred feet from his mother. She
     will remain for him a young woman

in a photograph. What draws us to the places where we were left behind?
     The boy's father slows down, driving by that barn,

a fiery-afternoon sun-red. Inside,
     uneven windows edge with dust, the dark of distant trunks.

Tools tilt and fall, the weight of rust,
     divided in light between floorboards.

He pictures swallows flitting against the ceiling. The way he took her
     around the corner when everyone had left, lifting

her thigh, cupping the back of her knee. Yes, where they prayed
     for the light to stay still in its quiver on the beam,

and for the sunset, like their heat, to emblazon them. What draws us to the places where we were left behind?

One Last Look at the Cathedral Pines

(My mother's voice before the tornado)

I need you to do exactly what I say:
Take your seatbelts off.
Get on the floor in front of your seat.
Hold your head over your knees.
We're going to be fine. Stay there.
Don't look up. I'll tell you when it's ok.

I always brought my girls with me
on photo shoots. This time, I thought
we would beat the storm. I asked
for a different lens, the camera bag
hanging from one of their small shoulders.

I yelled at my little girls —
Get away from the fence,
get inside the station wagon. Go.
I'm coming. Get in the car, girls, close the door —

(A different perspective)

We are 42 acres. We are old-growth white pine.
We are hemlock. We are centuries. We were purchased in 1883
to prevent logging. The tornado of 1989 destroyed us. We became
a study site for ecological restoration. We protected you
all those years.

(West Cornwall, Connecticut, the backseat)

I remember thinking those trees went on and up
forever and that they didn't have tops. I remember us,
in your Dad's '47 baby blue Citroen convertible, on our way
to the Village Memorial Day Parade, our hair wild
around us. Or at night, on the way to your house
for dinner, headlights and forest.

(I was born during a thunderstorm)

When I learned that tornadoes are born
in thunderstorms, it all made sense — the spinning,
swirling air of my life made sense. The rain stops —
white church — open stretch of road.

Tornado

The drama was not in the backwards-flying swerving
infant screaming tire screeching,
or the greenish-dark noon. Not
in her thinking

This is the last road. Someone might not find us up ahead.

It was not in the branch dent or drilling rain. Instead,
the drama flew at her in the form of a stranger,
a man falling to his knees
in relief on the kitchen floor.

It was his home. She was driving by
with her baby boy, and ran through the front door,
in from the storm,
windows shattering, and huddled

with his wife and child
until he could reach home.

Was there anyone in front of you? Maybe a van. I'm not sure.

Someone has rebuilt his shed, a swing set.
Both directions, fallen wires. The fire chief's voice again:

I need to know: do you remember any car in front of you?

Days later, she sees a desolate landscape,
jagged, humbled trees, a farmhouse.
A truck driver frowns at a brush fire. Indelible,
these clearings.

A half an hour before the storm struck,
she supported her son's waist at the top
of the slide. The day was tinted
a color she had never seen.

TWO

Elegies & Ireland

I basked in you: I loved you, helplessly, with a boundless, tongue-tied love.
And death doesn't prevent me from loving you. Besides, in my opinion, you aren't dead.
(I know dead people, and you are not dead.)

— FRANZ WRIGHT

Adam

With a tongue that didn't know
itself — lost animal — his mouth
opened — eyes squinted. Dimples

like our grandfather's but without
the agile body. Adam's hands
were pale — reaching always in the air —

a button, Arcturus. My friend's older brother
weighed more than she did —
hoisted his little sister on his shoulders.

Adam's muscular dystrophy
made this impossible — erased
strength and sinew.

Doctors thought he would live
to be fifteen (he lived to twenty-four).
Upper body swagger — wheelchair

backward rock — laughter unhinged.
The screen door slammed
those summer nights

until my mother fixed it. We flinched —
our eyes and ears expecting a sudden door
the way she expected his special school to call

daily. She waited until it came — a voice
telling her of his fever. We waited for his life
to unspin itself from the swing set chain.

I loved that rush, sneakers scuffing
a sandy oval until I sat steady—
my eyes adjusting. Oak tree—complete gold.

I knew my brother in the silences. Flecks
of silver mica peeling from stone. Meteor shower.
Black lake—empty bed. I remember

the first Christmas my mother
didn't hang his stocking. I watched
her pull it from light and ornament tangle

in the dented box that reached her waist—
shake it—fold it in half—and put it back.

Stay, My Little Boy by the Barn, One Overall Strap Dangling

Long underwear, sweat-drenched,
       freezes to the wooden deck rail.

Bent at the waist, one leg folds over the other, the silhouette
       of a man under ice.

The long underwear came in the mail boasting
       one hundred percent guaranteed protection

against cold, against the elements, against the way time wears
       everything away. The tag said the fabric would never

wear thin. Military Thermal Underwear and long johns, silk weight,
       heavy weight. That is what anyone on the receiving end would expect.

But what comes is never expected. It may have been lightweight,
       but this weight is too much to bear tonight under the moon

spreading across the snow. He'll be a Fourth of July firework ember
       falling into water. Every year passing.

*Major Steven Reich was on a rescue mission in Afghanistan when his
helicopter was shot down in 2005. All sixteen personnel on board perished.*

To My Living Wife

I did not know how to be dead
at the beginning. Someone came
to tell you right before
our child was born. The airplane
crashing, the force,
they must have said.

No sign of the plane, only
a glistening Chesapeake Bay.
You are too empty to forgive me.
I shout at the asphalt
the wheels never hit.

My love, a crippled animal
hides itself, heals itself alone. I see
you have joined the fog,
chestnut tree, November.
The branches have
what they need. To forgive me,
the water, the accident.

*My great uncle served on the USS Intrepid and was chief experimental
test pilot at Chance Vought Aircraft in the late 1940s. He was killed flying
an XF7U-1.*

Horizon Line

It's the same dream since I was seven. I wake up
remembering heavy air, rustling trees. It's July. My heart —
a heaviness lifts, the giant shape above me, hovering, a shadow
lowering. My childhood friend and her father stand next to me.
I am yelling, I knew it wasn't lost. They are in there. They are alive!

A psychologist and her patient sit side by side
in the monotone hum of a flight simulator.

Throttle, dial panel, cobalt horizon, expanding sea.
A tattooed peacock feather drifts up the right side

of a neck. The year is 2062. Humans don't fly planes
anymore. Simulators exist only for trauma recovery.

Planes do not crash. People forget to touch each other,
however. In an emergency landing, go easy on the thrust.

You understand you will never fly a real plane, yes?

"Goodnight, Malaysian Three Seven Zero."
I'm sorry, but it was so real. I saw the plane land.

As a child, she devoured stories — all speculation, fishermen
finding debris, search crews in the Southern Indian Ocean.

Try saying this now — "Good night,
Flight Three Seven Zero. Can you try that?"

John

Poetry is a spawn of the heart, webbing relentlessly
its cool contentions,
like spiders before daylight.

— JOHN ALMQUIST

Jazz-filled, he swung down cobblestone streets
in time with an East Boston childhood. My grandfather,
whose large hands played minor chords in deep taverns,

pulled turnips, baked bread. When I was a child,
his heart surrendered. We visited him in the hospital.
We brought him his favorite — peppermint

balls wrapped in silver — that melted on our tongues.
The year he died, I did not reach his waist, but stood
instead, as he squatted down, saying,

Here, I'm coming down to your level. See, we're the same size now.
I write to you, Grandfather, in a journal you began
to fill — story plots, scraps of dialogue, incidents

that compelled you to record, as if names and passions
might disappear. The quiet of tonight is the middle
of any February. I give you back winter.

Dried geranium petals twist and flatten between pages.
I wonder why you kept such small petals, why you wrote
about searching for Uncle Bill, his Princeton ring falling

through ice water after World War II, and you didn't mention
jagged metal or the ejection seat. In smudged pencil,
your handwriting: *The actors all go into the blank,*

but the skeletal white traces of the story blueprints forever
on my screen. In a blurry photograph, your handsome body
in a football jersey, number fifty-seven, square jawbone.

You kneel, your teammates fading back
into a washed-out image before the spectators arrive.

Sweet Gum Seed Pods

Sleepless, a body shifts
in my stomach, a fan
pulls strands of hair across my face.

I think of the sharp giving
and taking of a body, my brother,
the summer he died. The fever

of July is only a night's drive
away. Our hands
have lost their language.

What is the name of those pods I collected?
The tiny mouths of birds,
permanently open, crowded into a nest.

We hold on to what we can.
My son's hair is thick, golden,
a wilderness.

A Crackling

The water around the land around a lighthouse can only be filled with salt. And why am I saying tightrope, it was a rope swing, not in the brackish pond, but in a lake up the curved dirt road instead until a tinge of pink in the sky said thunder said lightning and a mother screamed at her son to get out of the water now. Mothers throughout all of time screaming at their sons to get out of the water. The saddest stories they have heard. Real mothers losing real sons. Squares quivering on the screen. An old film sparking and crackling and it's like that. My mother told me it felt like that, losing a son felt exactly like that, a sparking, a crackling, then nothing.

Dinner Party, 1983

February. Windows burn above snow.
Fields stretch away. I am six years old.

Like music, my brother's voice dives.
His arms flail around my parents' guests,
his hands alive with language.

My mother catches
all this, her Nikon lens in firelight
as if she knows.

A Field in the West of Ireland at Dusk

For Ariana

I picture you in ten years, in Ireland as I was at twenty.
Like mine, your voice may get caught

    in the marbles, spaces you have yet to discover,
    an electric fence turned on.

I was not in the half-stunning accidental photograph
you found and asked me about, not

    in the bedroom alone, watching shadows cross
    my body, not who anyone thought I was.

Two barred rock hens and a rooster vied for attention
on our farm this morning. They had mine.

    Field and fence, a blur of lines until we are made
    of fours: the fourth stone away from you in the stream,

the Fourth of July your sparkler set your hair on fire,
the fourth word you spoke. If someone looks at you

    a certain way, it is useless to pretend but you must,
    you absolutely must. Take anything from the night, daughter,

make it yours. This is it. Be mindful of the daffodils.
We are not going to be here again. Recall my cheekbone,

my lips pursed in the fading day, how your hair and my hair
and the forest become one. Right now, I am still a face

wanting to be known. I have so much to tell you,
while they call, looking back at me, from the island shore.

Division

My professor looks unmoved
by the woman across from him,
as he lifts a bay leaf from a cup
of carrot soup, lets it drip onto ink,
his last sentence about the self, divided.

Across the café from him, I watch him lift
a bay leaf. He tries to describe Siena,
its bluing night, lets it drip onto ink,
his last sentence about the self, divided.
She frowns. He stares into my corner,

divided. He tries to describe Siena.
How many times has she heard this one?
She frowns. He stares into my corner.
I look down. Tomorrow
he will recite Arnold, Tennyson.

How many times has she heard this one?
I will think he walked through
the nineteenth century. I look down. Tennyson,
tomorrow. My professor looks unmoved
by the woman with whom I imagine he walked

through the nineteenth century. I remember
a man in a film who flew out of a house
into a snow drift to cool desire. My professor looks
unmoved by the woman, by the bay leaf.
Now, see a snow drift as a way to cool desire.

What She Hears

A woman remembers Ireland,
hasn't been back since Gabriel.
In New Hampshire's deep winter,
a man's gone missing near
her property. She has decided
he is Gabriel, has imagined the scene,
combing her fingers through his hair,
kicking a log farther into the fire,
forgiving him. The news says
the missing man comes from outside
Boston, a football coach. The search
crew — his entire team, boys with their lives
before them — dig in the snow.
Inside her house, family members
sing, sip rum, tune fiddles, mandolins.
She walks the snowdrift alone. No sign
except a pickup, no stranger, no Gabriel.

Lost

A radiant woman peels a soaked leaf
from her neck, leans against me, restless. Death
is the thing that aches us into living, she says,

a watery distortion of Auden's line to Yeats:
Mad Ireland hurt you into poetry. Do not become
his Ophelia, I say. Remember her madness carried her

to that brook. Get on a late-night train
if you have to. The mountains seem more distant
than usual tonight, the air more arousing. I need

something out here. I need the dog barking
to remind me of a home somewhere, a bone
somewhere. I am trying to rebuild those tiny ships

we burnt last night. We lit each vessel, watched
their wooden bodies grow into colorful flames.
We were stunned, almost laughing

at the glistening water, the madness in our eyes.
Remember those tiny ships somehow,
if you can. As I walk away from you, part of me burns.

Meeting in Galway

We'd meet at half seven,
the pub on the corner with the bright
yellow door. "Last call, blokes." I'd follow him,
barrels rolling out,

past the canal, stacked for the taking.
On Saturdays, the smell of crepes
from the open market filled the town.
I bought thick candles and curry soup

with mustard seeds to hold and gently pop
between my teeth. We danced
to Tom Waits in a room with no furniture.
Rosie, how can I persuade?

We fell down one afternoon in hysterics,
trying to balance a mattress on our heads
along the canal. When I had a fever
and imagined a frenzy of white birds

in his room, he asked me about them
and held a cool washcloth to my cheek.
I imagined his older face. Twenty years,
and I smell that town, rain

and bricks of bog turf burning.
It was the same every night.
He was never the same
except in his transience.

Number 6, Lower Canal Road

After crossing the full river
I thumbed bread crumbs into tile grooves
across his kitchen counter. My toes
curled, body stiffened.

At evening lectures on Victorian prose,
we took notes, frantically covering every line
with script. I studied his black, scraggly hair
in front of me, his ink well,
a linen scarf loose about his neck.

We fell asleep beside a fireplace
in his room. He had been trying
to tell me about a woman
in Germany, waiting. I dreamed we pulled
nails out of a wooden floor together.

Shantalla Road

Through the ceiling,
two people share close
laughter. A silence.

Her voice wanes.
A flute urges night air
through the window.

Three notes, cut short,
staggered moan. I see
the two, his lips

slowly, clumsily, sliding
over the mouthpiece,
off the flute, falling

to her neck, collarbone.
We are made of this —
the anticipation of touch.

I wait for more music.
Instead, they roll, the flute
gently hitting the floor.

THREE

You & Me

The human heart is like a night bird. Silently waiting for something, and when the time comes, it flies straight toward it.

— HARUKI MURAKAMI

A Conversation with a Granddaughter I Imagine

Even if your voice splinters,
tell me what you can,
she pleads, this granddaughter.

Oh, she is the reflection
of Katharine Hepburn,
I think, just like my grandmother.

A lantern, rusted, hangs its fire
inside the barn. I'm not sure where
to begin. Maybe ask me

about when the lights of a hostel by a cliff
turned out to be the lights on a different island,
and how that meant I was lost,

the fast darkening sky. Or ask me about the heat wave,
the tall man stepping into an outdoor shower
made of upside-down blue-green glass bottles.

Your grandfather, I say, and close my eyes.
The handwriting! she cries, sifting
through my box of letters. I see each of them, she says,

the longing. I picture them writing to you
from coffee shops, train cars, park benches, Grandma.
No one is ever gone. May I read to you? I nod.

Let's see. Here, Maggie wrote: *I think you are adorable.*
And a man? a boy? wrote in summer: *Meanwhile,*
the wildflowers turn to drying seedpods

and the fish in the river grow. The air
is cool and we pick out constellations
and track Mars across the southern sky.

Did you ever wonder why
you didn't track Mars with him? Or did you?
From the same year, typed lines

from your grandfather's best friend,
about Adam's death. (Yes, I'm naming him.
I'm naming them all). He writes, *Your brother,*

as poetry tries to do, enhanced the mystery of life, enlarged it.
I wish I had known him, Grandma.
The first boy you loved, when you were twelve,

wrote to you at twenty saying, *If time*
and responsibility did not exist, I'd come
up to you and say, hey, do you want

a shiny blue bike? I want to know
which letters you tore in half.
I want to hear about him. Don't let your head

get in the way this time, wrote Katherine.
I want to ask if you took her advice.
I miss you. We just got snow, ten inches

is someone's way of signing off.
And your friend Em, a Skidmore friend?
wrote from France, describing stars

on the ceiling of the navy blue foyer
in her homestay home. *Make good art
and send me your poems,* she writes in ink,

the most gorgeous script I have ever seen,
black against mint-green paper. Have you come
upon Neal's writing yet? I ask.

Here's one. He wrote this: *I received an email from you
several weeks ago, and I had to leave the desk at work to be alone
with the beauty and strength of what you said.* And when you

lived in Galway, your grandmother wrote to you on paper
she called an aerogram. *Now they are called that,* she explained.
Letters like this used to be called v-mail. V as in victory,

written to overseas troops during World War Two.
It didn't take you long to join the soccer club, she writes,
marking her statements with exclamations.

In all of her letters, she seems so proud of you.
*Don't be lonely. Remember who you are. I hope the academics
are up to your standards.* Fragments from your father.

When you went to Ireland and they went to Spain and France,
you and your college roommates wrote to each other
with such adoration. One said she cried at the sound

of your voice from a pay phone. The same friend
recounted a boat ride like this: *The sky was still
that smoky early morning black.* They were all love letters.

All of them. Bridget covered the sticky side
of a piece of scotch tape with red glitter,
folded the tape in half, capturing

those tiny perpetual rubies for you.
That same Em who wrote from France
also sent you a tea bag, stapled it to a letter

with an arrow pointing to the bag reading,
Almond Sunset, your favorite. She wrote in the fall,
and you were home with Mono for two months.

*We had a critique in drawing class today. Yesterday
everything was mist. Drink water and sleep and I'll see you soon.*
Another friend, Jean, from County Clare, covered

her return address with gold paint, just light enough
to make out her postal code. And everyone wrote,
good luck and *be good* and *stay you.* I was buoyed

by their words, I say, or did I even know that then?
You tell me about a boy who wrote he'd see me over break,
and that was Charley, who fell asleep at the wheel

driving east with a friend. It was a semi. I held myself
up on a fireplace mantle, I remember, that Thanksgiving break.
I was twenty in an apartment, and my childhood friend

was gone. In these pages, all the remorse that could ever exist
in a soul. All of the love, too. Your father, he wrote,
Time will go quickly, but I want you to know that I miss you

already. Have a successful semester at University College Galway.
And your twin sister, apart from you for the first time
at twenty, wrote from Florence: *Get some vitamin C.*

I love you so much. During that same semester abroad,
your grandmother wrote, *Guess I won't be whole again
till you come home.* I close my eyes. Grandma. Listen.

This one, from Chris. Writing from Santa Fe,
he described building his own house, how he hoped
only to build once. *We received some good spring*

*rain which has helped relieve the drought, and I imagine
the creek below is full of clear water from melting snow.
I would love to come to your wedding*

if I can get back to the northeast. And your mother
wrote to you saying she was glad she planted you
in this galaxy. *Stay well*, someone wrote. *Call me when you return.*

If it hadn't been

for that tent
on the island,
our daughter
wouldn't be here.
If it hadn't been
for the avocado slices
in the rice bowl
and the ginger beer
in the frosty mug
a decade earlier,
I might not
have stayed
so long. It hadn't rained
half the day, and we
were out wiping
blue spruce shadows
from each other's bodies.
We have worked hard.
We were inevitable.

Off Center

A foghorn loses its regularity once
we fall asleep. Who is out there,

to hear it in the blurred dark?
A lobsterman has leaned

against fish crates for the night,
has cast off his waking life

for a dream that will be
interrupted. Early sunrise,

the clank of one pulley dangling
over the stern. In his sleep,

a white fence flashes
through wavy glass. Beyond,

he sees someone.
His young mother? No,

the girl he lost. Her skirt
screaming against the thick air.

Hunger

You see, it was hot orange light back in the forest by the rusted water tower where he said never turn this way, flames billowed, never want this way again. She couldn't make out his face through the woodsmoke and wasn't sure what it was but a hunger, the kind only a virgin knows. This was primal. This was two people staring at each other through swirling dust and slide projector light, an art history lecture twenty years ago. He watched her chip clay off a thumbnail, her rough hands. She searched for him during lectures, his five o'clock shadow. What if she had gone with him to the water tower? *Always make eye contact,* her mother had said. The thought of him looking at her, the rush at the start of the hundred-meter dash. You forget a word and suddenly, bright fields and graffiti walls flash past a train window, and you remember. That's what it's like. For a moment, a clear thought will arrive: I shouldn't want more. Take in another's face. No one will stop you. Afternoon glows a streak of gold across the glass. Brooklyn. Blue gathers between black buildings. Pink blur against glass. I ran back to you, ran the back of two fingers slowly along your face. As a child, you took in the galaxy within your room, glow-in-the-dark stars your father placed there one by one, knowing one day his son would know those winters were hiding something. Life unfolds, *becomes more gorgeous with time*, your mother will tell you, tucking you in. She believed this. The moment you name a longing it becomes a thing exposed. I wake in the middle of the night worrying you are stuck in a storm. In seventh grade, we left the dance, fumbled our way along the dirt path the way I have been fumbling through my talk of desire. On a night hike at twelve, our camp counselor handed each of us a wintergreen lifesaver, urged us to chew it with our mouths open, and to watch. Small sparks, specks of glowing mint, lightning in our mouths that had not yet been kissed.

Twenty-Three Years a Widow

His poems took her breath away, waiting
in an envelope for her on the other side
of the world, and it's as if I remember
my grandmother sweeping the stage
while he played the piano, moments
before they met. To my mother,

who is moving back into her childhood
home, I say, keep, at least in a box,
the chandelier pieces she coveted.
She never imagined she could live
without him. Keep the Cartier pocket watch
she designed for him there

on the mantle. What did she wear
to the premiere of that symphony
he wrote for her?
She called the dog down
the back hill every night as if calling
to people on the shoreline.

In a Different Life

I draw in a quick breath. The poet places his pen on the podium,
      looks up, then down, then reads. I think of the way heartache
      distorts as leaded glass.

      I think of the heartache I have caused. I think *Stop*.

Now, still, evening air rustles an oak. Are those trees
      ice-resistant really?

Think of two people in a tent
      who have been up all night, a thunderstorm wild

through them. *I will always listen to you*. You ache for this.
          There's a cold and barely discovered quarry. Meet me.

Scarlet Tanagers

and warblers

fly mostly at night.
Some migratory birds
cover nine thousand miles
to nest along the coast,
just to find their mate.

And look at us.

That winter those years ago,
the delivery was stuck in a storm.
A large truck, snow, a driver shivering,
with our love, a package of cracked
wire coating revealing the raw, the irreversible.

Oh, but it is reversible. We have proven this,
the way my heart jumps and proves I'm alive.
In dreams that I don't mean to have, I prove it again.
I put on my black velour coat. We're going out tonight,
yes, let's go out. Those birds make our yard

their wintering ground. Let's let them
and leave them on the quiet, snowy branch.

The freshness of the young couple
by the pond last summer.
Her hot pink bikini, the line
of his hip bone sloping.

Oh, that is us. Look at us.

Melt, April

The furnace clicks and thumps in our mud floor basement
like an old green Chevy shifting gears. At the top of the hill,
a driver squints, truck stalls, starts again. Our house, chipping
red, sits stubbornly, backdrop of forest. The place has seen hurt,

so much that its gutters filled with leaves and water and froze
that way. I think of other couples in our room long ago, biting
against the cold, exhausted, and here we are, naked beneath
beams, the black sky beyond and the stars. You have taken me

into your arms, back to our house, brown rice, warm bread.
You fix the furnace when it leaks, the gutter when it splits.
Now, with tape and scissors and glue, I am running uphill
alongside the truck. Wait. I need your help. I'm trying
to fix this. Let's sit by the road for a minute.

Marriage

He pulls, releases, pulls the cord
of his chainsaw. I try to say *restless*
as he reaches for the last breath
of the machine, races the light.

If it doesn't work, his plan to chop wood,
clear that corner of field, will combust.
I wear leather boots my sister brought back
from Italy — stylish, but not for this

New Hampshire winter. We have come
to the beginning and the end of it
many times, have skirted the thing.
Opposite poles might connect. Instead

we spin, magnets in the air,
quick circle of missing. A friend told me
how so much of life is about what is not.
I still have Ireland and that café, wine bottles

with candles dripping. I imagine dim light down
a hallway in the most majestic house.

Late August

The field flashes
through the stone
wall as I center
my body over
yours, brush
a black fly
off your hip.
Your hand
on my back
steadies us.
In the shade
by the fence
you built,
cicadas announce
the fall. Sheep
meander away
out of respect,
as if they
can hear. We
have made love
out here before,
but not like this,
never like this,
where each
gesture forgives,
each branch
above us aching
to be blown
against another.

Wedding Gift

The snowscape is oil paint
on canvas across a Vermont field
outside my friend's studio.
Four-by-four feet, it hangs
on my living room wall.

Its surface is pure white
from a distance, the way
my dress must have looked
to anyone outside the little church
looking in the open doors.

At the fitting, after handing
over my sketches — exactly
how I would like the straps
to widen gently at the shoulder
— I saw the color of the fabric,

the way the sky washes white over
pale yellow over white and the snow
becomes a shade of faraway blue.
Ten or more fence posts, buried.
A backdrop of brilliance.

While Reading a Jean Valentine Poem
in a Bookstore Café

A question breaks my quiet:
"Oh, you—did you
fall in love
the other night?"
Another woman gasps, catches
her friend's eye over
a shelf of Marvel graphic novels.
"No, no, I need to talk about it
with you." *Did you fall in love the other night?*
What does it mean—I wonder—
that upon hearing these words,
all I want is for these people,
all of them with their cappuccinos,
their craft beers, to think
of nothing but the last time
it happened to them.
Just write, everybody. Don't think,
I will say, and, hypnotically,
furiously, all their lovers will emerge,
the northern lights across the page.
Some of these people will sigh.
One will close his laptop, stare into space,
then open it and flurry across
the keys. I enter a small, sad state of shock
when I realize this absurdity
will not be. *At all costs, don't stop,*
I might exclaim. They have no reason
to trust me except,
Can we agree it's about longing, all of it?

The fire engine tea pot, the crystal-stemmed
ice cream cups. "So,
should I just keep it going
for now?" The women
by the bookshelf again.
"Yes, until it fizzles. Get what you can."
They laugh. I turn my eyes
back to Valentine,
get what I can.

It's Viable

All I can figure out
is that harvesting
may have ignited
something in him.
What if we all
announced our wants
more? He wrote:

The crop this year,
vines and fruit everywhere.
Please come home.
I can't wait
to drive you through
the covered bridge
again, at daybreak.
You'll drive me wild.
I'll pick you up
from the river studio
and we'll lie down
in a September canoe,
and drift. In my cabin,
we'll eat and drink
and I'll listen this time.

A Man on the Way to His Love

We follow the river's
curves. Sometimes we bend
and flow. Rows of long grass flash
as the train passes November.
They look like thick,
yellow pages turning.

Seven years ago, I saw you.
At first, you looked like birds
until the birds became leaves
swept upwards,
traversing cold air, and falling
to cover the silver top of a silo
across the river. Remember
the old man who raked wet leaves
on the sidewalk every night
as we walked past? I coveted
his satisfied expression.

The debris that falls
with rain, I am the vulnerable,
the dog-warmth.
Next to the silo,
a fallen-down barn
prepares me to change
as a shifting,
darkening sky.

Almost too old,
I am a chiseled, unshaven

face in the window tonight,
an Adam's apple sinking,
rising. I am still
the dog fumbling, tangled
in the chewed-up leash
around its legs.
I am almost in your city.

Duality

What they did with each other
was never our business.
The barn dance ended,
flannel shirt, sundress draped
over rock. Flustered,
she bared her shoulder.
I know why we didn't stop her

from making strangers
her lovers along the riverbank.
A different season
vanished the field.
Behind each of us
is what we will never admit,
except in the safety
of a firestorm in the privacy
of a dream, forgotten immediately.

If I Were a Filmmaker

They'd be laughing, exhausted, wrapped around each other
      all tan outside their orange-and-white '68 camper — the same
            summer

my grandmother begged them to move east. Sacramento, Baby. All
    those festivals,
        the boardwalk, short shorts, long hair. Everything

was out of this world. In New Hampshire, forty years later,
      my car stereo shares a static burst of promise:

European spacecraft Rosetta to catch a comet and land on its surface, and
    I think of my uncle
      now gone. I scroll through Instagram squares — repurposed

vintage vans, then look up how to care for a dying Juniper Bonsai,
      but all I can see is the two of them, propped

on their elbows, heads craned back, breathing in Jupiter.
      Listen: I know which house they found. It was false.

Forgive them, their youth. They trespassed. To think it all
      could last. I can't stop picturing the scene.

Specific Gravity

I carried you,
moved you,
wrapped
and unwrapped
you tightly
in headlines.
I kept you
there, stared
at you, aside
a kiln, all light
green, gold,
and charcoal.
My hands
fit your body
perfectly, every
thumb print.
At night, I go
to the studio
looking for you
or a version
of you, unfired,
bone-dry,
your most fragile
state, and I keep
wishing I'd known
the extent of it
as if I could
have kept you
on that shelf,
safe. Slip is exactly

as it sounds,
clay floating
in water, difficult
to grasp, but
what I would do
now. That cassette
I decided to keep
once when throwing
others away will
now live in the studio,
and I can't shake away
the fact that I'll never
be able to tell you
anything again.

Bioluminescence

What I am trying to say
is that I loved you with abandon.

A dory fisherman, his figure
against the dawn. I took in

every turn
        of his body.

Life tears and rebuilds when we sleep.

The jazz pianist made me walk
down Fifth Avenue ahead of him,

so he could watch. Hips, teal dress,
loose braid down my back, golden ribbon.

Asphalt, spark.
        It's not just phosphorescence.
        It's bioluminescence,

a marine biologist said to me
in a boat one night.

I knew every spine of every book
he ever taught.
        The sides of the dory

were chipping gold. It's a strange word

to end with, not *loved* but *ravaged*.
Almost all of this is the mind editorializing

what the body does, a beggar speaking
just behind me about his life,

saying, *You'll see.*

Or

you whisper to the singer:
    Listen for tonal energy.

A small opening in the theatre's curtain shows
the cocktail dress is the garment of the poem.

You will grasp at the idea of responsibility,
at the thought of him tugging gently at the hem.

This is the world we are dealing with.
Keep what you want to do

meticulously hidden. From the edge of the stage,
look at him. His eyes will crinkle at their outer corners.

Imagine Them Once

I.

Lightning and thoughts of you started a fire in the back field.
No, thoughts of you, not lightning, started the fire.

In a dream, I had to not care when a truck, fully consumed by flames,
rolled over the city dock into the harbor. I could not stop it

the way I cannot stop the sunflowers that push up above the field,
past the dark edge of woods, hitting the sky.

In the window shadow on my bedroom wall,
I found you. I spun your potter's wheel one more time.

II.

I wandered trails creating compositions with my hands,
always sure to keep off center

the object of my focus — a moving train, a moss bed, your face.
Empty barns at a distance cast their open-door light across

the purple snow. I hold one hundred and thirty years
in my left hand and touch the edge of you, a house resembling mine

in a vintage photograph, figures chopping wood in the foreground.
The cursive graphite reads, "Remember the good times on the creek,"

and I picture her now holding him, river ice bursting.
His arms wrap around her. Nothing can prepare us.

FOUR

Kaleidoscope

She had the bizarre feeling of time bending all around her, as though she was from the past reading about the future, or from the future reading about the past.

— MOHSIN HAMID

Warning

They say, and I know, it's like flying over
a large country, every field or city block
disappearing below. As if disapproving
of the morning, shake your head, golden fire.
Take it all back. I'm shaking my head at you.
What pleasure he took in distorting the color.
If a man walks you to the top of a hill
on the windiest, coldest January day, you risk
more than frostbite. They say this, and I know.
One day you will be an old woman
watching a film of yourself. It will be snowing.
You'll see when you fell for his words. Now,
picture theatres filled with people on the edges
of their seats, whispering, shouting
Make the right choice. So, these highway flares
are no more than a show. You drove
right past them. We all do.

Red Cape, c. 1788

Children died beneath
the slanted ceilings
of this house.

      Women carried kettles,
      lit oil lanterns,
      hung them against the wall.

Now early sun veins glow
across the shed's tin roof.
The tractor clunk-hums

      behind me, a morning rhythm
      like the sound of a mother
      running bath water.

I saw it on a boy,
a long red cape,
some Halloween in a dream

      years before I became
      a mother. Then I saw
      a childhood house, a maze

of closets fading,
and I moved north.
I left a floorboard murmur

      of adult voices, and I found
      my own hammering
      over two hundred years.

Point of Reference

Rattling all the way down Route Seven, you drove
that stone blue station wagon into the ground.

You said, "Let's meet between
I have no choice and I'll stay here with you

for a little while." We looked at letters cast in lead,
trays and trays, pretended that was our life.

I said I felt like a botanist who has grown tired
of naming ferns. I told you my attic smells of old papers,

guide books to North American plants,
their sweetening petals. You told me to sit down,

to be the one whose plants grow radiant as ghosts
in the sharpening dark, to see their gorgeous sprouting up.

You said change your point of reference, your cast
of ghosts. And I said let's pray for Jessie, who was shy

so I played with her in the sandbox. Pray for the man
who loves his cut timber more than his wife, and pray

for the woman who has not yet been kissed
on a thunderstorm summer porch.

What We Say to Ourselves During a Pandemic

Think of your hat, that bureau. Focus
on what's in front of you only, the mundane.

But I wore that hat last year in Golden Gate Park,
at a music festival in the late afternoon October sun.

And when you say focus, all I see is the cobalt
of the short-sleeved silk and sequin shirt

I used to take from my mother's closet, shimmer in it
around her bedroom, and return it to its hanger,

a gosling growing into its soft wings. All I can think about
is the audacity of this afternoon light bringing me

to earlier times. The shifting green beyond
the ladder leaning against that tree. I'll focus on that.

Then crisp snap peas in the palms
of my grandfather's large hands, whir of boots

against tall grass edging his vegetable garden
up the back hill. If we are racing out of the water

to avoid the undertow, then aren't we always risking
it all? The thought of you is a lovely

interruption, the slur of sleep and dream. Stay.
I remember the cookies you baked for us,

how we called them Elephant Ears because of their shape,
sugar coating our lips. If you can, tell me she will be alright.

I am looking in front of me now, sun hat,
oak drawers, the rooster out my bedroom window.

Try some more focus. *Memorize the moment,*
is what she would say. *Mom, you will get better. Don't be afraid.*

My dad, thirty-nine years the head of a boarding school, will finish
his career at the end of a virtual spring term. I picture volumes

of yearbooks on his shelves, and lilacs out his study window.
A student writes to him from overseas, *Dear Sir,*

it should make sense to shake your hand one more time. I am writing
this email to you in case nothing goes our way. My father responds,

Your potential is without limits. He shares a story of overcoming
an illness while in college. *We will get through this ordeal,* my father writes,

but not without sacrifice. When my parents were a little older than you,
an entire generation shipped off to war, delaying educations,

leaving loved ones. He mentions a popular song in those days called
"We'll meet again." *We'll meet again, dear student. We'll meet again.*

Waiting

for Christina

Through the woods across
a field across the road
from my house, a train shakes
the trees like a load of wash.

My family has everything
but the lake here, and we believe
in a clean slate here. A jagged
piece from other woods tells us
from the kitchen wall in white
chalk which animals ran through
here. My twin sister waits

for a baby girl, an hour's drive.
A baby girl. I pace the floorboards.
I remember each creak, each river.
Nothing will mess with my sister's heart.
My niece arrives. The days shine
with sharp clarity. The nights
hint at fall.

Aphelion

A night sky quivering
is a trick of the eye.

Atmospheric turbulence
is meeting someone

at the wrong time —
shaking apart.

Explorers have found
the calmest place on earth —

top of the mountain,
bottom of the world.

We can't go there,
but we can dream.

We can imagine
a constellation

that never
touches the horizon.

Come Here

The cardinal
slams itself against
the front window

even when it rains.
You are nudging garlic
through beet greens

in a cast-iron skillet,
and I remember
an artist in a shed,

his studio, the door
opening to sunlight.
I grew up without

television. He grew up
without sight. For
a living, he shapes

wood into spoons
and small bowls.
"Let parts of your world

speak to each other,"
he said to me or
to himself. "I know

where you are." I
thought I was perceptive
until I found

that photograph
from fourteen years
ago, of the artist. On

the great porch
of that house
by the water, we tried

to catch lanterns
as they blew, hitting
their paper roundness

against the ceiling.
Across from the province
is the mainland.

Across the lawn,
I see a woman
from Iceland

claiming to have
never seen a firefly.
This drive has become

everything I can't say
to you. In slow, half-moon
strokes, I will

wipe your face
with a warm cloth.
This is all I can promise.

What She Might Have Said

When I was your age, the boys
over at the inn on Saturday nights
winked at me, lined up for a swivel.
That's right. They lined up

Just to twirl me around
the reception hall. The inn
was a place transformed those nights.
When I was your age, I didn't hem

and haw, gazing into my closet, because
my mother told me what to wear —
always a swing dance dress
she'd sewn, with bright trimming,

and a look from Jimmy O'Brien
was all I had time for
in those delicate moments
after the dance, on the terrace,

in the rain, as I waited for my ride
to drive along the lake road
to retrieve me. Those nights,
in the dark car with my father.

He called me his Jeanne,
couldn't stand the way it seemed
I might leave soon. When I was
your age, time was mine.

Turn, It's Been Three Decades

Scorched meadow. Can we watch it? Can we sleep
facing the fire tonight? Please, can we? you ask.

If I could have traced my finger gently in circles
along your skin forever, girls, if I could have.

"Draw on my back," you said. "Draw on my back.
I'll guess." One of you asked,

"A house? No, a forest with no house, no, no, wait.
A river? A storm? Am I right?" I would say yes

but be tracing a story instead that crashes and catches
itself in the current, one you may never hear, a branch,

released, sharp and torn to turn and float, splintered,
splintering, spinning, these years, in the summer's

river current. You will remember her face. You
fell asleep inches from it. I picture you

as seven-year-olds now whispering *Turn the other way*
so you could draw with your fingers again. You'll hold

someone someday, girls, their arms around you,
hands clasped at your lower back. A day like this

in your narrative will come. The field won't be burning.
It's ok. I'm right here. Your life will be a story.

It's time. Come in from the rain, girls.

Black Scarf

I would like to meet you
here on the Lower East Side.
You're in Panama, my love,
photographing Ruby-topaz
hummingbirds and Dusky
Nightjars in the heat. I am not looking
at the tall man who orders Chardonnay.

This small table has been worn
down to paler layers of paint,
wax-dripped, coffee-ringed
wood, elbow touch. The man
faces Canal Street. I wonder
if he held someone this morning.

A blue candle beside his bed
has lumped, spilt like a small waterfall
of glue, or ink, a torn beginning,
demolished town. Maybe
he is an actor who cooks for himself,
spoons lentils, potatoes, and fennel

into a pot on the stove. I want that man
to come back down the street. Why
do we accept that we are strangers
to one another? Should we have
exchanged more — the glow
of the glass by the window, the boys
and basketballs, the ancient light

of morning? I want the scarf left
on the chair to be his. It hangs
spontaneously in front of me.
I would run through the gray to him.

Before

Before dusk, before I registered the scene,
I'm on the line. 911 What's your emergency?
The line — between gasping — and my house
is not on fire, my kids are fine. I'm driving south
on 95, man on a bridge as I pass below.
His rock climber stance, a chain link Spider Man.
Someone just called this in. Same guy.
Thank you, Ma'am. I picture officers striding
the white line, the scaling man squinting.
They are rushing in my daydream, and they make it.
They coax him down. I have to believe this.
I cannot fathom a fence of sorrow
with no holes to reach in and bend open.

Lean In

Silhouettes against a bonfire pull me closer
until someone says, leaning in,

It's grand to have a mind, but it's hard to have a heart.
Did you see that mountain today,
the way it went gold, shadowed,
and turned the color of slate?

The way a Dutch woman on a train told me
she did not fear getting old. Never once.

Or the way my professor said, *Don't miss this.*
Don't miss this. A different woman between
Madison and Park, looked at me before
she disappeared, turned and said,

You must see the Macy's Flower Show someday.

We hold on to these lines, these lives
we'll never know, these lines and lives
we overhear. A wildness of lines,
dramatic light of lives.

Moonstone

If I could, I'd press my thumb along you
like I do across this smooth moon necklace
I want to hold at a distance, the way the moon

looks when I turn the usual dog walk
into something more and I round the barn,
and stand to see it, enormous, and astonishingly low

upon the horizon. The kind of moon that could light up
a fifty-acre field. I am skipping stones in the Vermont quarry
where my friend took me when we were nineteen

and visiting her family's Cabot home where the flood
filled the field and her father rowed a boat across it. *The greenhouse
is flooding.* A person admitting that he needs help can be beautiful,

but very much like when I notice the moon has already slid away
and down. I don't run fast enough into the house to grab my camera.
The seconds adjusting the lens and I miss it.

Medium Format Photograph

At the wedding, they wear daisies to match their daughter's crown. They reach out as if about to waltz, as if about to say, *Stay here.* They could not have known they only had five years, could not have predicted the gin and tonic glass in the hand of the man in the background would shatter. The woman in the vertical-striped Marimekko dress would scream until they took her to a room with one small window. These two stand there grounded for now. Will you stay?

The North Woods

Last night, I heard from them outside,
not past loves, but a chorus of tree frogs singing
to a different world.

Stay steady. Breathe deeply. We're here.

"Here's to your health," says the man with the chronic illness.
What else makes sense to say? Fifteen years ago, a crescendo
of glances, this same man's arm brushing against mine

as I stepped outside the log cabin. I walked up against
the North Woods and listened.

We were there years later but couldn't protect you.
The river sparkles in sunlight but will eventually go black.

At the end of an avenue somewhere, a lamp flickers.

You Say

If you raise chickens, then you know. You say
you've lived a New England winter? You know.
But did you know we are all running this way
and that, our wishbones not snapping yet,
holding good luck in still. Holding still.
Good luck. If you recall, she hung the delicate bones
on a metal hook about to overflow.

A Novelist at the Trailhead Makes a
Story Out of Strangers

What that woman might lose: his hands on her back.
What that man might lose: clarity of mind, agility. *This illness*

messed with the wrong body, is a conviction worn like a bald tire
flirting with rain. But they say it. A lightning storm could split

their house, could rip the balsam firs to shreds. They have to believe
some forecasts are faulty. They don't need to know the barn's on fire

on Kodak paper, or the exact lines of their longing will shift.
She tells her children "You cannot singe some details away.

You'll reach each log yourselves. We'll readjust then,
and only then. I hope this couple has years.

Before Us

My husband hammers
the heads of ancient nails
into our hardwood floors,
smoothing the ground
for the baby. Beyond

the shed, beyond
the sheep field, he left
a rake, a tin bucket looped
on a fence post. Beyond
all the stone walls, a trail

curves through these acres
of forest and I hear the voices
of a family, their five children
buried in the graveyard, names
on one headstone, their deaths

days apart. The walls
of my son's bedroom
are a pale yellow
I painted a year before
he was born.

February, New England

That I haven't cried in ten months tells me
a winter storm takes it upon itself to completely cover
a wooden walkway, leaving steps indiscernible,
altering landscapes. That I won't let myself

reminds me, when I was twelve, my parents could run
a hand along my temple at bedtime, but not get stories
out of me. My favorite sensation
is having my back scratched.

See, I need shoveling, a blade to chip away ice.
I should be crying about the actual frozen river dam,
the one that stopped time in that town. Anger tightens
our bodies. I'd rather watch this snow.

Stonehouse Pond

Come ready with sturdy hiking shoes, ready to catch
and release. These wetlands and woodlands will leave you
breathless. You'll leave no trace. Let's review the rules:

Floating: encouraged
Entrance fee: no
Swimming: yes
Exploring: yes
Paddle boarding: absolutely, a must
Bathing: no
Finding inner peace: unavoidable

Come ready to cast your line, raise binoculars to your face.
Focus. Don't look away except to adjust your footing
on a rock or a root. Stand still. Stay still. Come swim,

see light and color flash against water below a granite cliff,
all 150 feet, on the pond's southwestern shore. Anglers, hikers,
cross-country skiers, trappers — you're all welcome.

No motor boat touches the water's surface. Eastern
Brook trout fill the 55-foot depth instead. Blue Gill, Chain Pickerel,
too. If you're paying attention, you'll see a map. The map's legend

will tell you in symbols of Shrub-emergent wetlands, vernal pools.
The property line will be a dash, an important mark of clarity.
You'll see a symbol for a gravel road, and another for a gate,

trail, footpath, and bridge. Come ready to the ridge
and use caution. Use caution all the way around, but not so much
that you miss the Mountain Laurel patch, the perennial stream,

or the beaver dam. Over three-hundred-year-old black gum trees
will surround you, shelter you. Come ready. Come wild
like the water's edge, like the sky at sundown. You know the rules.

The Middle

I have to be willing to get this wrong.
My mother used to say, *Would you rather*

be right or happy? The stubborn
sixteen-year-old, the one I can reach

back to still, would think but not say
I want to be right. But I'm talking

about race now. Is it too easy
to say I should not talk now?

What about silence? My instinct: to listen.
My other instinct: to say, can we please

discuss this? I will put down my boxing gloves.
In fact, I never had any. I won't say

I know how you feel. I don't. What is the purpose
of writing and hashing it out? What if writing

is the thing that makes us keenly aware, and if
we never become aware, from where

does empathy pull into town? Or am I just
taking up space? What does it look like

to meet a person in the middle
of the night — the middle of understanding?

First Cousins Visiting

It is dusk. We are on the dock, taking off
ice skates. We are children — orange-fuchsia
afternoon, frozen Lake Waramaug — as we trudge

up the driveway like last night when your parents
carried you, crisp starlight, up the stairs to bed,
in from the car from the airport from the plane

from your California sun. Action figures,
coloring books spilling from your backpacks.
When he followed your mother to Santa Cruz

in the seventies, he stayed, and back east during visits,
in the still, early morning, he sat in Grandma's kitchen,
the only two awake. Every time it stirred a sparkler

in her, filling her with stories. When I picture your father now,
he is showing you how to build a fortress inside yourself, how
to be tender men. Last Spring, he let my daughter reach up

her hands, stand on his feet, and he danced her down
a different driveway. That scene — uncle, daughter,
cousins, lake — returns to me, glinting pink-gold.

Abroad

If we went there now, knowing
    how we pretend
    and forget,
    would the night street fair
    look the same?

Could we still be anyone?

A world away
    from a rainy Paris night
    when anything was possible.

Chimneys smoked
    and our hearts skipped a beat
    in that country.

It was time
for a stranger's kiss.

Tangle

2 a.m. phone call, kiss your wife
    on her hairline, your baby's face flushed
    after nursing. See your other boy asleep. Dress
    in armor, lock the safe.

In the next town over, a man panics at the sirens
    and throws a loaded gun instead of himself
    in the lake. You have seven hours

before the children arrive to swim. Four hours, no gun.
    You determine how deep a child can swim
    before freezing. The gun goes deeper,
    falls fast through branch and black.

For Ben

Let's hold
every spring
we've ever
lived. Daylight
rounds the corner
now, orange
in the silver
wind chime.
Look at me.
There's a movie
in my mouth.
There are scenes
I need you to see.
We're in there.
No, not through
the door, right here
in my mouth.
Our heads
are thrown back,
see? You
are making me laugh.
Let's not ever
forget to look
again
and again,
at each other.

Free Advice

If you mistake the taillights of an idling van for the window glow of a hostel, wait for the traffic signal to change, watch the red reflecting off wet road, let the tires disappear over the hill, keep walking. If you need a place to stay tonight, this might just be the wrong town, wrong time. If you believe I don't remember your face, I'll tell you now, I would know it in the dark. Maybe I'll meet you in the dark, but you have to keep walking for now. Think of the gestures we all misread, slough them off, step over them. Keep going.

NOTES

p. 4: "Northbound 35" by Jeffrey Foucault (*Stripping Cane*, Signature Sounds, 2004)

p. 11: "that it takes half a century to figure out who they are, our real true loves" was inspired by a line in "Washing the Elephant" by Barbara Ras (*The Last Skin*, Penguin Books, 2010)

p. 35: "Goodnight, Malaysian Three Seven Zero" (the last radio message sent from the cockpit of Malaysian Airline Flight MH370, March 8, 2014)

p. 36: "Poetry is a Spawn of the Heart" (original poem by the late John Almquist)

p. 37: "The actors all go into the blank, but the skeletal white traces of the story blueprints forever on my screen" (a notebook, my grandfather, John Almquist)

p. 45: "Mad Ireland hurt you into poetry" (a line from "In Memory of W. B. Yeats" from *Another Time* by W. H. Auden, Random House, 1940)

p. 46: "Rosie" by Tom Waits (*Closing Time*, 1973, Asylum Records)

ACKNOWLEDGMENTS

Grateful acknowledgment is made to the editors of the following publications in which these poems, sometimes as earlier versions, first appeared: *Hamilton Stone Review; The Café Review; Oakland Review; Port-smith; Off the Coast; December Magazine; The Hunger Journal; The Coil; The Concord Saunterer; North American Review; Driftwood Press; Lunation; BODY; 2River; Inklette; Currents V; Raleigh Review; Clockhouse Literary Magazine;* and *Bellingham Review*

To Paul Marion at Loom Press, for your kindness, your keen eye, and your genuine attention to every letter and space.

To Dennis Ludvino for your elegant design work.

To my students, current and past: You are pure gold. You challenge & inspire me.

To my teaching colleagues: You make me want to be better at what I do every day. You amaze me.

To my own fearless and devoted teachers. Your impact has been profound. To my teachers at Washington Montessori School who taught me to love the written word; Pat Jones, my first creative writing teacher at Hotchkiss who helped me begin to find my voice; Geoff Marchant on the soccer field & Marjorie Reid in the art studio—both of you helped me find self-assurance. Sarah Goodwin, Barry Goldensohn, & Marc Woodworth at Skidmore: Thank you for helping me nurture my love of language during my college years and for being role models to me in direct ways.

My deepest thank you to the Program for Writers at Warren Wilson College, and especially my unparalleled mentors, Debra Albery, David Baker, Mary Leader, and Gaby Calvocoressi.

To the following organizations & people: National University of Ireland, Galway; Breadloaf Writers Conference; New York State Summer Writers Institute (Carolyn Forché & the late Lucie Brock-Broido); Twin Farms Writers Workshop; Susan Schulman; City Hall Poets, Time to Write Workshop; Poets House; The Word Barn & Word Barn Meadow patrons, performers, and readers.

A special thank you to these friends and mentors who have supported me and helped me keep writing at the forefront of my life: Tim Horvath; David Rivard; my dear Titia Bozuwa; Zoe Lasden-Lyman; Sara Katz; Kaitlyn MacDonald; Seth Pollins; Katherine Rand; Patrick Pate; Nathan McClain; Jenna Baillar-geon; John Kucich; Mercy Carbonell; Bridget Devine; Jen Evans; Reginald Dwayne Betts; Elisabeth Waterston; Jen Onken; Lilly Robers; Meg Day; and the late Tony Hoagland.

To Matt Miller for your steadfast friendship in poetry. To Sean Singer, David Rigsbee, April Ossmann, & Maggie Dietz, for being meticulous early readers of this collection. To Heather Allen for believing in me as a poet since I was a child.

To my family, I adore you.

To Mom, for nurturing self-expression from the start, for being the best photographer and the most loving mother.

To Tom, for leading by example with your creative mind, keen design sense, and enviable teaching skills.

To Dad, for reminding me with every facet of you to be confident, to trust myself, and to work hard.

To my grandparents & Adam: You are all very much still here.

Christina: My twin, my muse, my moon magic. I am blessed by our bond.

Aengus & Ariana: you are the poems about which I am the proudest.

Ben: Thank you for laughing with me and for listening, for challenging me when I need it, and for being tender when I need that.

Author Photo: Jennifer Almquist

ABOUT THE AUTHOR

Sarah Alcott Anderson holds a BA in English from Skidmore College and an MFA in poetry from the Program for Writers at Warren Wilson College. Her poems have appeared in *North American Review, Raleigh Review, December Magazine*, and other journals. A high school English teacher for eighteen years, she chairs the English Department at Berwick Academy in southern Maine. With her husband and two children, she runs the Word Barn, a gathering space in New Hampshire for literary and musical events, including writing workshops and her reading series, The Silo Series.